You Are A *Virtuous Woman:*

This is your identity.

R. N. CALDERON

"Loving God Enough to Experience This with You"

Copyright © 2014 by R. N. Calderon

You Are A Virtuous Woman
This is your identity.
by R. N. Calderon

Printed in the United States of America

ISBN 9781498421362

All rights reserved solely by the author. The author guarantees all contents are original and do not infringe upon the legal rights of any other person or work. No part of this book may be reproduced in any form without the permission of the author. The views expressed in this book are not necessarily those of the publisher.

Scripture quotations taken from The Message (MSG). Copyright © 1993, 1994, 1995, 1996, 2000, 2001, 2002. Used by permission of NavPress Publishing Group. Used by permission. All rights reserved

Scripture quotations taken from the English Standard Version (ESV). Copyright © 2001 by Crossway, a publishing ministry of Good News Publishers. Used by permission. All rights reserved.

Scripture quotations taken from the King James Version (KJV) – *public domain*

Scripture quotations taken from the New International Version (NIV). Copyright © 1973, 1978, 1984, 2011 by Biblica, Inc.™. Used by permission. All rights reserved worldwide. www.zondervan.com The "NIV" and "New International Version" are trademarks registered in the United States Patent and Trademark Office by Biblica, Inc.™

www.xulonpress.com

Contents

Introduction ix

Proverbs 31:10 13
Proverbs 31:11 15
Proverbs 31:12 17
Proverbs 31:13 19
Proverbs 31:14 19
Proverbs 31:15 23
Proverbs 31:16 26
Proverbs 31:17 30
Proverbs 31:18 — Part 1 35
Proverbs 31:18 — Part 2 39
Proverbs 31:18 — Part 3 43
Proverbs 31:19 49
Proverbs 31:20 53
Proverbs 31:21 57
Proverbs 31:22 61
Proverbs 31:23 65
Proverbs 31:24 71
Proverbs 31:25 76
Proverbs 31:26 80

Proverbs 31:27 84
Proverbs 31:28 88
Proverbs 31:29 91
Proverbs 31:30 95
Proverbs 31:31 99

Dedicated to the Virtuous Women who are uninformed.

Thank you to my Brothers and Sisters in Christ, who weren't afraid to do what the Lord said concerning me.

To My Mighty Man of God, thank you! Above all, thank you God, my Father.

Introduction

Oh yes, you shaped me first inside, then out; you formed me in my mother's womb.

I thank you, High God—you're breathtaking!

Body and soul, I am marvelously made!

I worship in adoration—what a creation!

You know me inside and out, you know every bone in my body;

You know exactly how I was made, bit by bit, how I was sculpted from nothing into something.

Like an open book, you watched me grow from conception to birth; all the stages of my life were spread out before you,

The days of my life all prepared before I'd even lived one day.

—Psalm 139:13–16 MSG

In this passage, the writer realizes God has nothing but good thoughts and plans for his life. As I read it, I realized that I was unsure as to what my identity was, but all paths lead back to the word of God. God has already taken the time to speak life into who we are as women. God already knew that you and I would need to understand how to be a woman in this world. As my journey started with gaining a better understanding of the Virtuous Woman as described in Proverbs 31, I began to realize that if God does not lie, then everything in this passage is true about me, too. I just need to figure out how to "tap" into what is already deposited in me. When God made you, God also gave you that same virtue. The thing is, we as women have not always been taught how to properly use it.

Too often people say, "Well read your Bible and pray about it, girl … You need to pray harder, come to church, and worship with the people." But the reality is that sometimes you need a person to be real with you and to show you how—and not just hope that if you read the Bible, you will get it. Now don't get me wrong: I know my God is able to do anything, but I believe when He says it is good for us to fellowship with one another.

"So let's do it—full of belief, confident that we're presentable inside and out. Let's keep a firm grip on the promises that keep us going. He always keeps his word. Let's see how inventive we can be in encouraging love and helping out, not avoiding worshiping together as some do but spurring each other on, especially as we see the big Day approaching."
—Hebrews 10:22–25 MSG

This includes sharing our life stories about how God helped us through with one another. Therefore, this is where I take my life testimony and share it with you so you can also claim your victory to then share with others. This is how we win souls for Christ, not condemning them but loving them.

As you embark on this journey of your identity as woman, more importantly a Virtuous Woman of God, I pray God gives you what you need in order to make it through this part of your life.

*****

Proverbs 31:10

"A wife of noble character who can find? She is worth far more than rubies."
                    —Proverbs 31:10 KJV

During this time, rubies were valued as we value diamonds today. God is the first to tell you that you are "a ten," that you are precious, that you are worth beyond your weight in gold. God already did all that first. So any man who comes into your life now has to be able to love you with the love of God in order to even begin to understand your worth and treat you as such, in addition to being the man you need in order to bring glory to God's kingdom. You already know God has a call on your life, and when we don't take the proper steps to work toward that calling, nothing feels right.

How would you care for a ruby if you had one?

You Are A Virtuous Woman

As of right now, you are not allowed to forget you are a virtuous woman. Starting right now, when life happens, before you do what is easy, remind yourself that you are a new creation in Christ Jesus and you are virtuous. Then you can handle the situation. Don't take your ruby and rub it in the dirt; keep it in high places away from all the mess.

*****

Proverbs 31:11

"Her husband has full confidence in her and lacks nothing of value."
                              —Proverbs 31:11

Change the word "husband" to "God," and read it again:

"God has full confidence in you and lacks nothing of value."

God *values our praise*.

God has full confidence in you and doesn't lack your praise. In this race we have to praise. For me, it started with the little things we take for granted. I thanked God every time my children upset me, and I said out loud, "God I thank you for my children because there are some women who can't have children." Then I made it a habit to pray with the girls in the morning before they went to school. We started our prayers off with thanking God, then praying for others and then for ourselves, thanking Him for all He has done and will do.

When we start to thank God continuously for the small things, God will provide the big things. Before I knew it, I was praying every time we passed an accident on the road.

Don't focus on your problem; just be aware it is there. Focus on God and all He has surrounded you with. The crazy thing is, even though we are going through something, we still have to be about our Father's work. As soon as you start to see God, and move when he tells you to, then we can do like the passage says at verse 25, "She is clothed with strength and dignity; she can laugh at the days to come."

Start today with praise, and take it with you everywhere you go. God, I thank you for the work you have begun in us.

*****

Proverbs 31:12

"She brings him good, not harm, all the days of her life."

— Proverbs 31:12

It never ceases to amaze me on how God gives us instructions if we will only seek them. This verse is like the summary of what is about to come as we study Proverbs 30:10 – 31. It reminds me of just what it says. We are to bring Him (God, our Husband) good and not harm all the days of my, and your lives. This is to let you know up front that this task is not temporary; it is very much continuous. As long as you have made up your mind to be this woman God has called you to be, you have to know all it entails. Without a doubt you have been equipped to handle it. As we have been told before, God will never give you more than you can bear.

At this point, please know that you will have to make some changes; some people in your life are not going to be able to take this journey with you. You already know who you need to let go of, and now it just time to do it. You will be surprised at how good you will feel once it is done. It is better to part ways with someone when God tells you than to try to hold on to them. You would be in turmoil until you finally did it.

We are not perfect; however, I know you have the desire, and God is pleased with that desire. Now we just have to take our desire and put it into action, one step at a time.

Let's bring God good, not harm, all the days of our lives. I love you, and I look forward to seeing you later.

*****

Proverbs 31:13-14

"She selects wool and flax and works with eager hands. She is like the merchant ships, bringing her food from afar."
—Proverbs 31:13-14

"She seeketh wool, and flax, and worketh willingly with her hands. She is like the merchants' ships; she bringeth her food from afar."
—Proverbs 31:13-14 KJV

Now let's put this in modern terms. God is telling us we can shop! Just keep in mind who we answer to, after we bring all this stuff home. We still have to be good stewards over what God has given us. Let's break it down...

We are responsible to ensure our families (and we ourselves) are properly clothed and fed. We need to buy healthy food, and we don't have to always make a quick meal. We should sometimes take the time and effort to prepare a well-balanced meal. Not only should we prepare meals, but also we should be eager and willing to do so.

We shouldn't be in the habit of saying "I don't know if I'm going to have enough money to get that this week" when it is something we need, like bread, milk, eggs, a hat, gloves, shoes for the children, and so on because we are responsible for what God has given us. Let's dig a little bit more. Because I love you I'm going to help ensure our understanding.

All passages, found on www.Biblegateway.com

"Whatever you do, work at it with all your heart, as working for the Lord, not for human masters,"
—Colossians 3:23

"And whatsoever ye do, do [it] heartily, as to the Lord, and not unto men;"
—Colossians 3:23 KJV

You shouldn't be trying to keep up with the Jones's, such as "She got a new____, so we need to get a new____, or "I want people to think I am____ so I have to ____." God says clear as day, *you need not do anything to seek the approval of man*. It's all about bringing glory to our Father—your works should be meeting His approval. You can't please both God and people, so "choose you this day who you will serve" (Josh. 24:14–15). We already know that not everyone is going to be able to travel this road with you. If you lose some folks along the way as my Auntie says "... and it is still well." If man doesn't approve of you living for God our Father who has kept you, then bless them very much and send them on their way.

"Keep your life free from love of money, and be content with what you have, for he has said, "I will never leave you nor forsake you" (Hebrews 13:5). As I read this, what came to mind was this: the woman makes the clothes, but the clothes don't make the woman. If God has blessed you to where you can afford all the name brands and still be able to handle all your other priorities, then great. But if God has blessed you so that Goodwill is more in your price range and you still be able to handle your other obligations, then you need to be right there.

"Show yourself in all respects to be a model of good works, and in your teaching show integrity, dignity" (Titus 2:7). Never forget, someone is always watching you, you who say you are a Christian, a Virtuous Woman.

Your children are smarter than you give them credit for. If you set your priorities backward and are not taking care of your obligations, what you think you are grooming your legacy to do? "This is how one should regard us, as servants of Christ and stewards of the mysteries of God" (1 Cor. 4:1).

All the information given to you here are tools to aid you in your journey. However, above all, remember that God will give you direction if you seek it from Him. The next time you purchase something, ask yourself, "How this bringing glory to the Kingdom of God? How is this benefitting my home?" Am I saying not to splurge every now and then? No, I am saying take care of business, and God will make a way for the splurge.

So let's shop for good clothes and go grocery shopping for good food to ensure that we are well fit to serve a Might God.

*****

Proverbs 31:15

"She gets up while it is still night; she provides food for her family and portions for her female servants."

—Proverbs 31:15

This verse starts out saying "She gets up while it is still night ..." I love this verse. When God wakes me up early in the morning before my normal time, it seems like those are my best days because that's when I take the time out to just spend time, me and God. This is all about acknowledging God in all his goodness. Sometimes, God just wants to know if you hear Him. When we have bad dreams and you wake up out of your dream, tell God and thank Him for saving you from the nightmare. Then ask Him to cover you and your family while you sleep. It brings a new meaning to the idea that we should always be in prayer.

Next, let's consider, "She provides food for her family and portions for her female servants." This is time invested. We may often find ourselves rushing, but the reality is that God has given us all the time we need to do everything we need. Where do you place your priority, concerning what needs to get done in a day? We have time for reality TV and sports, talking on the phone, or making up for the sleep we didn't get last night. We as women, as mothers, and wives should always be ready. Ready for what you ask? We should be ready for the unexpected. We know that God will never give you more than you can bear. However, what are you doing to prepare for the unexpected?

Remember when you neglected to do something and then, when the other things happened, you wished you had done that one thing? Okay, let's do it like this: Matthew 25:1–13 talks about the ten virgins. Half of them weren't ready, and the other half was — read about it. If you read further in the chapter, it will give you some more good examples.

God doesn't set you up to fail; it is the opposite. He sets you up to succeed, and we choose not to take the proper steps to be ready. Back in Bible times, not only was the woman of the house responsible for making sure her family's needs were met, but also the needs of her servants, as well. To put it in our terms, is your family ready? When you go to work, have you done all you need to do to ensure those whom you are responsible for are ready? I'm not saying you have to force people to do things your way, but I am saying that you should make sure you have done all you need to do to equip them properly. Are you setting the example which allows other to draw from you what is needed to prepare them for the unexpected?

The next time you wake up an hour earlier than normal, thank God for waking you up before time (you have to start small). Once you make this a habit, you will start praying your way back to sleep. Then you will begin to pray your way into your whole day.

*****

Proverbs 31:16

"She considers a field and buys it; out of her earnings she plants a vineyard."
—Proverbs 31:16

"She looks over a field and buys it, then, with money she's put aside, plants a garden."
—Proverbs 31:16 MSG

How are your investments benefiting you as a whole? Yep, let it sink in, I'll give you one hint I'm not talking about investing money.

How is reality television benefiting you? How is dating just to get out the house beneficial? TMZ? Spending money you don't have? Sitting on the couch? Living on Facebook/ Twitter/ Instagram minding everybody else's business but your own? How is not being about God's business benefitting you?

In Proverbs 31:16, the Virtuous Woman is investing her time to go out and scout a field.

I imagine it's like house hunting or searching the stores for a sale. Time is invested, then the decision is made, and then you maintain your home in a manner which will benefit you in the long run. Once you have invested your time in something, do you know how it benefits you?

I remember when I started watching a reality TV show, *The Real House Wives of ...* during my downtime. I was watching a marathon of the show, and by the next day I was acting like one of the ladies from the show. For a week, I was acting like this person. Then finally, a friend said something to me about it. I couldn't believe it; this lady was very unladylike in my eyes, but I had picked up her mannerisms.

Let's talk about the one we all can relate to ... social media. You got those "friends" who continually post drama, and it seems like they just mess up your day. If they don't make you sad, you are at least frustrated with their stupidity (by the way: it's time to cut them off). Yet you subject yourself to the mess for hours on end. How are these things we dedicate so much time to bringing glory to God's Kingdom? Please believe me, I know social media can be used to glorify the body of Christ. It's just that nine times out of ten, we aren't doing it. William Shakespeare said "The eyes and ears are the gateway to your soul," so what are you allowing to enter your soul? Is it things of God? You can only give people what is in you. So if you allow wretched, hot mess, negativity into your soul, then guess what: you will have no issues doing the same things. Yes, you will have no problem being wretched, a hot mess, and negative.

If your desire is to be God's Virtuous Woman, you need to keep your mind on spiritual things; the word says "You (God will) keep him (you) in perfect peace whose mind is stayed on you (God), because he (you) trust in you (God)."
—Isaiah 26:3 ESV (explanations added)

Make a point to invest ten minutes with God daily, however the Lord leads you (i.e., talking to God in prayer, reading the word, reading the *Daily Bread* or other devotional), and watch things in your life begin to shift.

For me, the improvement was in my stress levels: my children's father didn't bother me, work wasn't dragging me down, and I learned to stop trying to fix other peoples issues.

What do you have to lose? "Taste and see that the Lord is good; blessed is the one who takes refuge in him" Psalm 34:8

*****

Proverbs 31:17

"She girded her loins with strength, and strengthened her arms."
—Proverbs 31:17 KJV

Even as I began to write for this scripture verse, God was working in me. I hope you are ready. Let's break it down…

In other words, she prepares her body with the power of resisting attack and becomes stronger to endure bravely or quietly. How are you preparing your body to resist attacks and to be strong enough to endure bravely or quietly?

God desires that we be in good health. Believe it or not, society does not have the final say in this area. As a child of God, we have to know He has already placed people where they need to be in order to help us along the way. For example, I believe God has made provisions for doctors. With all the knowledge

God has allowed them to acquire, they are here to assist you in being in good health.

In addition to this provision, God has also equipped us with the ability to stay healthy. God is not asking for much—take a walk every now and then. Park your car a little ways back and walk into the store. God didn't say you had to join a gym in order to be healthy. However, if that is what will motivate you, then get on it. It really is simple, we just have to invest the time in doing so. Even in all my health issues, I still manage to walk, and during the time I am walking, I talk to God about everything, and nothing at all. I want God to know my voice so that when I call right now, I don't sound like a stranger to Him—and I want to know His voice, too. Do what God has equipped you to do in order to keep your body in good health.

Which leads us to into this ... She develops a firm and unwavering character, with the power of resisting attack, and she becomes stronger to endure bravely or quietly. How are we developing a firm and unwavering character, with the power to resist attack, becoming stronger to endure bravely or quietly? Yes, you guessed it. God needs us to stand firm in His word, and to be unwavering in it.

You know when Mr. Man is touching on you, and your flesh is feeling oh-so-right and you manage to say, "I want to wait." But then he starts kissing you on that spot on your neck ... Oh, that's just me—okay.

How about when you are laying lonely in the bed and you want Mr. Man to come lay with you, but you know if he does you will have sex—Oh, okay, so I'm the only one who has been single and horny; that's cool. I'm still going to tell you God wants us to be unwavering. I have learned there is so much glory, honor, and peace in maintaining your virtue.

Let try this, how about when your friends try to talk you into doing something you know God has delivered you from, whether it is smoking, clubbing (maybe you're too old anyway), or drinking. When you find yourself around a certain type of people, all of a sudden you start cursing. You start excusing your kids from the room because you don't want them to see what you doing or what your friends are doing. No, it was just me ...?

Well, I'm going to say it anyway: God says He has already equipped us to have a firm and unwavering character. We just have to tap into it with God's help, praying something like, "God, this man is making me feel some kind of way, but I desire to be the women you have called me to be. God, I don't know how I got here, but I desire to do better." God will make a way for you. God knows your heart, but He needs your actions and your words to follow.

Will you be perfect tomorrow? No, but with the help of God, you can take steps to being better than you are today. Will you mess up along the way? *Yes*, but as you make the decision to move the way God tells you to, your mistakes will be few along this journey.

Remember I told you that William Shakespeare said, "The eyes and ear are the gateway to your soul"? Well God our Father in His word said, "Faith comes by hearing ..." (Rom. 10:17). What are you listening to? Is it of God?

"Therefore, get rid of all moral filth and the evil that is so prevalent and humbly accept the word planted in you, which can save you.

Do not merely listen to the word, and so deceive yourselves. Do what it says"

—James 1:21–22

By doing such, you are preparing our bodies and developing a firm and unwavering character with the power to resist attack and to become stronger, enduring bravely or quietly.

*****

Proverbs 31:18 — Part 1

"She sees that her trading is profitable, and her lamp does not go out at night"
—Proverbs 31:18

"She perceiveth that her merchandise is good: her candle goeth not out by night."
—Proverbs 31:18 KJV

The Virtuous Woman sees that her calling is profitable, and her grace (God's calling in your life) is not sinful.

God has called your name and you answered. You have decided: "I want to be Christ like; I want to be a Christian. I desire to be a Virtuous Woman." So here is where you have to truly understand and believe that this life you have chosen is good.

Jeremiah 29:11 says, "For I know the plans I have for you," declares the Lord, plans to prosper you and not to harm you, plans to give you hope and a future."

I like the way the King James Version puts it "For I know the thoughts that I think toward you, saith the Lord, thoughts of peace, and not of evil, to give you an expected end." This version reminds me that God will be there until my end. So from day one, God had decided it would peace for us. All God asks in return is that we commit our lives to Him. Really, is this a difficult decision to make?

Are you reading this and the thought crossed your mind that you have been slipping on the Christian thing? Or, you have been going through the motions and your heart wasn't in it? Did you tell yourself that you are mad at God because you did something wrong, and you know it was wrong—and God let you feel some of the consequences of your actions? Well, the great thing about God our Father is that He forgives us. All we have to do is ask. So right here right now, let's pray. I even dare you to say it out loud, exercising your faith now.

God,

I'm sorry; please forgive me. I need you to help me turn my life around. God, I surrender it all to you. If you find anything in me that is not like you, I ask that you take it away from me because I desire to please you and to be the Virtuous Woman you have called me to be.

And from this moment forward, I will actively make steps to do your will. Amen.

Understand, if you truly want to do better, God has forgiven you. So forgive yourself and make moves toward doing God's will. God has a plan for our lives, and it does not matter how long it takes for us to get it. If we truly seek His face, He will perform His work in us as we allow Him to order our steps. This is your training; make a choice to practice and chose to work repeatedly at being a Christian until you are proficient in those things in which God has called you to do.

You can't get better; things won't get better if you don't continue to practice. Get yourself a coach or spiritual mentor by asking God to help you discern who would be good to assist you in this area of your life. Then get you some teammates, who are people who are like-minded who will encourage you and remind you that you are not going through this journey alone.

I like how the Message Bible says it in Proverbs 27:17–18:

"You use steel to sharpen steel, and one friend sharpens another.

If you care for your orchard, you'll enjoy its fruit; if you honor your boss, you'll be honored."

What you genuinely do for a friend, you will benefit with them. Even if it's not them returning the favor, God will ensure you reap what you have sown. They will also pray for you like your mentor does. And yes, you need to pray that God shows you who can be a part of the team. The Bible is how you get trained: Basic Instructions Before Leaving Earth. Putting what you have learned to use is how you become skilled.

Enjoy this moment with God as you have been placed back on the right path. Surround yourself with people who have the same desire as you do—to please God. Get around people who are positive, those who know how to pray. Most of all, pray for yourself; your ministry starts at home with you.

*****

Proverbs 31:18 — Part 2

She sees that her trading is profitable, and her lamp does not go out at night.
>   —Proverbs 31:18

She perceiveth that her merchandise is good: her candle goeth not out by night.
>   —Proverbs 31:18 KJV

The Virtuous Woman sees that her job is profitable, and her grace is not threatened.

In whatever you do, do it to please the Lord. We have made it this far, and at the least, we know God is almighty. When you are in the workplace whether we knew this or not, we are working for Him. Hear me when I say, *we are still working for God, and we need to bring glory to His Kingdom*; this is your profit. When you are at work, people are watching you and talking about you. Don't confuse your confidence with conceit because there is a fine line between them. In your confidence, remain humble. Jesus in all His glory still was a servant to the people. No, He didn't let people run over Him. However, Jesus didn't walk around with an "S" on His chest. Jesus let His actions speak for Him. There is no need to voice who you are and how great your works are because, when it is true and genuine, others will sing your praises.

Next time you have to go to work, pretend like God is going to stop by your desk. Park your car like God is going to park right next to you. Ever notice how executives park? They park in a way that seems like perfection. You know why, right? It is because they can't afford to let their subordinates think negatively about them. When you start to interact with your co-workers, customers, and upper management, act as if the Angel Gabriel and the Holy Spirit are your co-workers, Jesus is your supervisor, and God is the owner. What report would you want them to give concerning you?

Newsflash: even when you are at your place of employment you are being a witness for our Lord God. If you look like you have an attitude every time a person walks past, if you are quick to point out the problem before a solution, if you show up to work looking crazy, tell me how you are setting yourself apart from others? How is acting like this bringing glory to the Kingdom?

Even the Bible talks about how you should maintain yourself in fasting and praying.

When people look at you, they should think you are kept safe in God's hands beyond measure and your life is good. You shouldn't give them a reason to fill the need to get involved in your life. Stop telling folks how you are going through this, that, and the other, and you still making it. All you are doing is boasting about yourself in the eyes of others. This is one of the biggest lies we tell because the reality is that we aren't making it. God is carrying us through, and without His guidance, we are lost.

When they see you, looking like you are on top of the world and they ask you how you are, give God His glory. Tell them the Lord is keeping you; tell them you are blessed and highly favored. I know when you say these things you are glorifying God and may even be drawing those around you closer to God.

As women we sometimes get the short end of the stick in the workplace only because we have been made with grace (femininity). While we may be more qualified, men seem to be dominating. It seems we have to work harder at times, but we can rest in knowing that God is on our side. As we continue to be the women God has called us to be, and we continue to stand up right before our Father, God will keep us in the workplace and we have no reason to feel our grace is being threatened.

Have you ever met a lady who is in a manly career, like an auto mechanic? More often than not the lady begins to take on the mannerisms of the men around her. But when we let go and let God, we don't have to conform because God will keep our grace intact.

The position you hold within your workforce is not about you. It is your opportunity to give God the glory by different means. I'm not saying shout and break out dancing every day, but I am saying not to leave God in your car when you come to work. Bring Him in with you and keep your grace intact.

*****

Proverbs 31:18 — Part 3

She sees that her trading is profitable, and her lamp does not go out at night
—Proverbs 31:18

She perceiveth that her merchandise is good: her candle goeth not out by night.
—Proverbs 31:18 KJV

She sees that her walk of life is profitable, and her grace is not deceiving. Is your grace deceiving? Are you quick to tell someone, "Don't take my kindness for weakness?" I know it came out my mouth quickly, and I'm still working on it. Have you ever really thought about how that sounds? It sounds like we are saying if someone attempts to take advantage of us, then we will do something not holy. Really think about it. Normally when this comes out of your mouth or you hear someone else say it, they either have or are on the verge of having an attitude. If you're like me, I roll my eyes and shake my head, and it's really bad if I get to giggling while all of this is going on. But that is just me.

However, my grace is deceiving. I'm really nice and holy until you cross me, and then Sister Calderon has become that B*(@# Calderon. Don't worry; plan to keep it real. Jesus didn't say "I'm cool with you as long as you don't spit on me"; Jesus didn't say "I'll only show you love as long as you don't nail me to the cross." He didn't say "Take on the consequences of your own sins because, really, I didn't do anything wrong and yet I died for your wrongs."

Even in the midst of all He went through, He prayed for us, "Father, forgive them, for they do not know what they are doing" (Luke 23:34). His grace was not deceiving. And even until today God is still showing us love.

I hear the old folks say, "If they nailed Jesus to the cross, what do you think people will do to you?" Why, ladies, are we shocked and surprised when people do us wrong? Brace yourself; it's coming straight—no chaser ...

When you have slept with the man you knew was either married or had a girlfriend and now he is cheating on you, why you mad? When you slept with the ole boy and you ended up pregnant and now he is acting like you trapped him, why you mad?

Is your Grace deceiving? Oh no ... we're not down your block yet?

How about when you were dressing like, a guy could drop a dollar and by the time it hit the floor, your clothes would be off? (not fully clothed) When you try to be a Christian lady on the street but a whore in the club, why are you mad when they talk about you?

Is your Grace deceiving? Still not you? Okay ...

When you lied to get what you wanted, talked bad about someone in order to make yourself look good, when you talked about the ole girl because she somehow gave you the impression that she was better than you, you just had to find something wrong with her and nail her to the wall (Jesus on the cross) for it. When you give someone the impression that you are friends, but when they need you to pray and stand with them, you bail because it's too much for you (or you think it might be too much for them, as well). Or the more famous one is when you say nothing at all, but your (my) face says a thousand words and when the person approaches you, the fake jumps out.

Is your Grace deceiving when you yell and scream at your children, but you seem to be

Mary Poppins with other kids or when you show love to your niece and nephew better than you do your own?

Is your Grace deceiving?

See that your walk of life is profitable—to you and the Kingdom. When you choose to live the life God has called you to and when we choose to be the Virtuous Woman God has called us to be, it is. We need to understand that our walk of life has profit—profit to us for our obedience and profit to the Kingdom because we are being a witness to how good God is.

For I know the plans I have for you," declares the Lord, "plans to prosper you and not to harm you, plans to give you hope and a future.
—Jeremiah 29:11

God is telling us he plans to help us prosper if only we would do His will.

No one will be able to stand against you all the days of your life. As I was with Moses, so I will be with you; I will never leave you nor forsake you
—Joshua 1:5

Do you know what Moses was able to accomplish what he did because he did what

God told him to do? God promises you are not alone because He is always there every step of the way.

You use steel to sharpen steel, and one friend sharpens another. If you care for your orchard, you'll enjoy its fruit; if you honor your boss, you'll be honored.
— Proverbs 27:17–18 MSG

Even when you start to feel like God is not there, God allows us to have people here on earth who have the same goals as you and me. God will send His Spirit of comfort and peace in a human form for those times when you need it. *This is not to replace God,* but He will allow it from time to time.

"When you fast, do not look somber as the hypocrites do, for they disfigure their faces to show others they are fasting. Truly I tell you, they have received their reward in full. But when you fast, put oil on your head and wash your face, so that it will not be obvious to others that you are fasting, but only to your Father, who is unseen; and your Father, who sees what is done in secret, will reward you."
— Matthew 6:16–18

God even cares about your appearance when you are doing His will, and since we ought to always be in His will, we should always be presentable.

Jesus said, "Father, forgive them, for they do not know what they are doing" (Luke 23:34). Even when people do you wrong, cover them in prayer—not in angry prayer but genuine prayer. Pray for you first so you can forgive and then for them, even if they never ask for it. Releasing the hold the devil tries to place on you is called forgiveness. Then, let God fight your battle. "Do not touch my anointed ones; do my prophets no harm" (1 Chron. 16: 22). God will handle your light weight.

This is how we ensure your grace is not deceiving and how we profit the Kingdom. I pray that God will continues to strengthen us as we strive to stand upright before Him and desire to be Virtuous Women. I encourage you to read 1 Chronicles 16:8–27 MSG.

In Romans 8:31, What, then, shall we say in response to these things? If God is for us, who can be against us? The God reminds us in Romans 8:37 "more than conquerors."

*****

Proverbs 31:19

"In her hand she holds the distaff and grasps the spindle with her fingers."
—Proverbs 31:19

*I*n her tenderness, she embraces family and understands the reality among her members. Stay with me, we as the "new age women" tend to make things harder on ourselves than need be. God has given us families for a reason. You have the one you were born into, you have the one you created, you have the one which is not blood, and you have your church.

So let's begin by understanding as a Virtuous Woman that you have been called to embrace your family. Most importantly, *love* them ... *yes* ... all of them, including the uncle who is always drunk, the auntie who always in your business, the cousin who steals, the jealous sister because she can't seem to get right, the dad who wasn't there, and the mom you may wish wasn't yours. The list may go on. Family is the tool God gave you in order to help you deal with the people out in this world who don't know you. Think about it; for everyone who is in your family against whom you have something against, there is someone who is not a part of your family who is similar. Therefore, if you are loving the characters in your family, it should be a breeze to love the ones who aren't if for no other reason than because God said you have to.

Show tenderness even to the ones who have hurt you the most. We make things hard because we try our best not to embrace the tools God has given us by way of our families. Don't forget: if God is for you, then who can be against you? That includes those who are close to you, as well.

I have come to realize my family are people who care about me enough to tell me what I don't want to hear. They keep it real, nine times out of ten. They don't even know they are telling it to me. Sometimes God makes them move because I refuse to just listen to Him.

Take it one step further, the reality is that your family is everyone. Because I love you so much, I'm going to let you know showing love means you need to possess and display the fruit of the spirit.

But the fruit of the Spirit is love, joy, peace, patience, kindness, goodness, faithfulness, gentleness, self-control; against such things there is no law.
— Galatians 5:22–23 ESV

When you possess and display these characteristics, God will set the rest in order.

In her tenderness she embraces family and understands the reality among her members. What is the reality among your members? The reality—yes, I recognize that some of them are not the best but they are still family—is that some of them will never get it right. However, you still keep them in prayer and operate in love towards them because just that quick it could be you. Love the addict in your family because it maybe be the love of Christ displayed by you that turns their life around.

Don't give up on the body of Christ; they are human just like you. The church family that hurt you and you are still carrying around the pain ... *Let it go*! Let it go right now, not for them but for you; don't let Satan win. When we walk in unforgiveness, we are taking a step in the wrong direction. When you give room for evil to creep in, it will somehow fester in your heart, and every time you see, hear of, or hear the name of whoever and however, your being is distraught. Is it really worth investing all that energy into the nonsense that benefits you absolutely nothing?

None of this is accomplished without God, so when you surround yourself in the spirit of God and you move as he guides you to do so, then you can be the instrument needed to bring about the change. "Ladies, you have been called to change the atmosphere (Rev. Marie Manigault). Forgiveness can only be accomplished through the love of God.

*****

Proverbs 31:20

She opens her arms to the poor and extends her hands to the needy.
—Proverbs 31:20

Now when you first read this verse, what did you automatically think when you saw "poor"? Someone who doesn't have money, right? So what about the word "needy"? The first thing I think is someone who is lacking stuff and money. Okay, maybe it's just me, so let take these words and look at them in a different light.

Here it is ...

She initiates her support to those lacking normal or adequate supply, and increases her giving to those who want affection, attention, or emotional support. Wow that just hit me hard. Let's go.

You know the person who keeps looking for "attention"? The one who feels the need to say the most random of things for no other reason than to be heard? You know, the one who talks just to hear the sound of their voice? Oh wait, how about the person who feels the need to tell a story that tops whatever someone else just said?

Okay, how about when someone get bad news and looks like they could use a hug? What about the person you passed by and you got the urge to say "Good Morning," but you didn't? What about the urge to say a kind word, but you don't say anything?

Don't worry; yeah, I'm guilty as charged. But God says we are built to support those who are lacking, whether it be attention, affection, or emotional support, and, yeah, sometimes money. The word *initiate* means no one has to tell you to do you just do. You see the need, confirm you can fill the need, and do so. How do you confirm that you can fill a need? The Holy Spirit will help you discern whether or not you can be of assistance. This is why we need to stay in constant communication with God our Father so when He does speak to us, we hear and respond appropriately.

Now note that I'm not saying God wants us to be nosey, but I am saying that God doesn't make mistakes. If you get the feeling to give money to certain people in need, God will give the same confirmation as to whom you need to provide support.

There will be times in which giving of your funds will be required. However, God requires us to use the love He has instilled in us so others may draw closer to Him and the Kingdom of Heaven. Let us not forget that all that we do is to glorify the Kingdom of God.

We can also tie this in to verse 19 concerning family; we may need to be the one who initiates the change in how we deal with the members who are shunned. Again, understand that everyone you come in contact with is family on one level or another. And for every one whose path you cross, God requires us to show love.

Choosing to be a Virtuous Woman will not be appealing to everyone. Please know it's okay. Those who can't get with the program and support you in this lifestyle of following Christ aren't the ones who you want around you. Just by acknowledging there is more God requires of you, and striving to meet those requirements, further confirms that you have been called to change the atmosphere. You are unique and as you continue to meditate on God's word, you will see He has already equipped us to handle this thing we call life.

*****

Proverbs 31:21

When it snows, she has no fear for her household; for all of them are clothed in scarlet.
—Proverbs 31:21 KJV

Now at first glance, you will interpret this that when the winter months come your family should have all of the winter clothes needed to survive the winter. Yes, make sure your family is good to go, but let's look at this from a different angle. So when trials come she has no reason . . . What are you doing to ensure your household is clothed in the blood of Jesus?

"Finally, be strong in the Lord and in his mighty power. Put on the full armor of God, so that you can take your stand against the devil's schemes. For our struggle is not against flesh and blood, but against the rulers, against the authorities, against the powers of this dark world and against the spiritual forces of evil in the heavenly realms. Therefore put on the full armor of God, so that when the day of evil comes, you may be able to stand your ground, and after you have done everything, to stand.

Stand firm then, with the belt of truth buckled around your waist, with the breastplate of righteousness in place (You have to be truthful not just to you, but to those around you.),

and with your feet fitted with the readiness that comes from the gospel of peace."
—Ephesians 6:10–15

You have to be ready, and the only way to prepare is when you study God's word and work your faith.

In addition to all this, take up the shield of faith, with which you can extinguish all the flaming arrows of the evil one. (You got to have faith),

"Take the helmet of salvation and the sword of the Spirit, which is the word of God."
—Ephesians 6:16–17

Your salvation comes from you establishing your relationship with God.

"That if you confess with your mouth the Lord Jesus and believe in your heart that God has raised Him from the dead, you will be saved. For with the heart one believes unto righteousness, and with the mouth confession is made unto salvation."
—Romans 10:9–13 NKJV

"And pray in the Spirit on all occasions with all kinds of prayers and requests. With this in mind, be alert and always keep on praying for all the Lord's people. Pray also for me, that whenever I speak, words may be given me so that I will fearlessly make known the mystery of the gospel, for which I am an ambassador in chains. Pray that I may declare it fearlessly, as I should."
—Ephesians 6:18–20

This right here is the kicker; you have to pray for those who are in the position to deliver God's word. Yes, you should be praying for me for I believe I have been entrusted to deliver God's word. Pray for the pastor and his wife; pray for those who teach Sunday school, Bible study: the ministerial staff. You should be praying for all your brothers and sisters in Christ, including yourself, because at any time we can be ordered to deliver the word of God by one means or another.

When you put all these pieces together, you have no reason to fear, for the Virtuous Woman is clothed in the Blood of Jesus.

*****

Proverbs 31:22

She makes tapestry for herself; her clothing is fine linen and purple.

—Proverbs 31:22

She guards herself from attacks, and her covering is sufficient and excellent. She covers herself; her clothing meets the need of a situation and looks magnificent.

Let's deal with the easy one first: She covers herself; her clothing meets the need of a situation and looks magnificent.

Plain and simple your body should be covered; there is no need or reason why the world should see the crack of your butt. There is no reason for your clothes to be so tight that the world can see your cellulite. You are a Woman of Virtue. It has been said, just by the way we dress and represent ourselves, that man decides how to approach or even if they are going to approach us. What kind of attention, what level of respect, is our clothing demanding?

Now I have never been liked for what I'm about to say, but I know I 'm led to say it anyway. If you dress like a hooker, why are you mad because you are being treated like such? When you present yourself like hors d'oeuvres (finger food), then what you are looking for is a quickie. But when you dress like you are a gourmet dinner, you will get someone who will sit down and take their time.

On to the next one ... She guards herself from attacks, and her covering is sufficient and excellent.

She is *you;* attacks are the things of the enemy; your covering is *God our Father*. You are to guard yourself from the attack of the enemy. Yeah, here it is again—you need to have *an active* relationship with God. Too often, we get saved, and then we stop there. That is where we go wrong; you have to be active. What do you consider active? Well let's go to the word.

"Study to shew thyself approved unto God, a workman that needeth not to be ashamed, rightly dividing the word of truth."
—2 Timothy 2:15 KJV

We need to read the word of God. Start out by praying that God opens your heart and your mind to receive what He has for you in His word. Every time I read a passage I have read before, I get something different. Have a dictionary nearby because you may need to look up a word you don't know.

"Even so faith, if it hath not works, is dead, being alone."
—James 2:17 KJV

Read James 2:14–26 for the full story.

Prove to God that you believe what He said. Start by saying you are *blessed* and *highly favored*. When you continue to say something over and over, you begin to believe it. It becomes a part of you. Remember life and death are in the power of our tongue, so speak life.

In a previous verse we discussed putting on the full armor of God and staying in prayer. We need to realize we have to make a conscious effort to maintain a relationship with God.

What would be considered actively maintaining a relationship?

Reading the *Daily Bread* and saying a prayer of thanks in the morning when you wake up and saying the Our Father Prayer when you lay to rest.

Act as though God were your husband—when you wake up, you would tell your husband good morning and when you go to sleep you would tell him good night. Say it to God. When you need something or when you are about to do something, you would talk it over with your husband. So talk it over with God. When you make decisions, you would take into consideration how it would affect your family, so consider how it would affect your relationship with God. Will it be something which would question your grace?

Just in case you haven't noticed it. I have been placing a lot of emphasis on your relationship with God. This is because without God, nothing will work.

"Therefore, my dear friends, as you have always obeyed—not only in my presence, but now much more in my absence—continue to work out your salvation with fear and trembling, 13 for it is God who works in you to will and to act in order to fulfill his good purpose."
—Philippians 2:12–13

*****

Proverbs 31:23

"Her husband is respected at the city gate, where he takes his seat among the elders of the land."

—Proverbs 31:23

*Y*our husband, the man you give your time to, should be a man after God's own heart. If he is not, then you are wasting your time. If after the first month you can't figure it out, bring him to church. If he is not for you church will reveal it because the devil isn't going to sit up in the house of the Lord too long before acting up. "Pray on and take Him to the King" (Tamela Mann). Yeah, we think we want a man who blends in with the guys, but that's wrong; you want a guy who strives to be like Christ. If that is what you are opening your eyes to, then the rest will fall in place.

Now if we believe what God says He wants for us, then we should believe a man of

God is good for us. Stop looking at what job he has right now; stop looking at how big his apartment is. Seriously, even if he is staying with his mother, it doesn't mean he's not a man of God.

I looked up the word *respect* and this is what God gave me: Her husband is appreciated at the city gate. People see the potential and motivation in him; others can't deny he has been set apart from the rest. Her husband is valued at the city gate.

People see he is worth something, not his possessions but his character, what he stands for, what he believes, and what he demonstrates. Let's not forget what we have all heard before: his actions speak louder than his words, and the two will not contradict the other.

Her husband is loved (the object of attachment, devotion, or admiration — Merriam-Webster) at the city gate. People around him will have a level of devotion or commitment to him, not as god but because of the God in him. It's been said, God is love. So if he is genuinely *loved*, then we should believe God is all over his life, and he is kept by Him.

Her husband is reliable at the city gate. You should know you can depend on him; others will vouch for him because they depend on him.

Her husband is look up to at the city gate. He is admired, not idolized but admired. And in this he will give God the glory. Your husband will recognize he didn't do it on his own, and nothing but the blood of Jesus kept him.

Her husband is acknowledged at the city gate. He is not overlooked, in the right city he is not overlooked. Now if you are on the corner, and the other men keeping passing over Marcus because he is small and scrawny and won't make a move but they keep him around to pick on, that doesn't mean you should aim for the one who has the teardrops on his face.

But if you are in the city where there are other Godly men, and you see that same scrawny man and the elders in the church are grooming him and he is taking heed to it the best of his ability, that may be the kind of man for you. Please understand there are bad ones in the church house as well. But since we have developed a relationship with God, we know to pay attention to the Holy Spirit. Do like me every time I let man accompany me to church; I ask the men in my church about him. And they will let you know.

More often than not as women of God, when our man comes to us, he has a foundation in God. But he is in need of values we offer as being women of God. Don't assume because he is not dressed in the latest and greatest that he can't be for you. Yes God knows what you want, and He will give you what you need. Sometime in order to get what you want, you have to put some work into it. It's okay to be with a man you have a vision for but it hasn't come into fruition yet. But if you stand by him and encourage him and show yourself to be in it through thick and thin, when God gives him the fruits of his labor you will be blessed as well.

Her husband has a high opinion of at the city gate. His opinion will hold weight and be taken into consideration. Even if they don't follow it to the fullest, he will have the respect to at least speak on the matter.

Her husband is followed at the city gate. To be a good leader you have to know how to follow; there is no getting around that. So the elder will follow him. If he is being led by God and they see the potential, they will follow him and advise him along the way.

He takes his seat among the elders of the land. What city are you looking in for your man? What city is he respected in? Who are the elders of the land?

The trick question is that it was already said "when a man finds a wife." So you not looking for him, but you are so immersed in

Christ that your husband will go to God to get you. Think of it as him asking God whether he can date you.

But what city do you find yourself in? What are you surrounding yourself with?

When you have been delivered from something, let's just use clubbing, and God delivers you, so ask God to send you your husband. Should you really go back to clubbing…?

I mean I know God can do it, but what are you willing to sacrifice while you wait? How much more time did you add on to your husband being sent to you because you find yourself back in what God delivered you from. Don't just pray God to send you a good man, but pray God prepares you for the God man. Your good man may not want you out in the club, drinking for the sake of drinking. He may not want you to be the life of the party all the time. He may not want you to be the one who feels like she needs to have male friends. Which really means that more often than not if we have men around us for no good reason other than friendship, it is *highly* possible that two out of five of those guy friends have feelings for you. I don't know your story; I'm just telling mine. And they will never admit it until you get a man and things start changing. All of a sudden he doesn't understand why he can't just take you to dinner. Ladies, we are responsible for maintaining the distance. Don't be smiling up in Joey's face and always calling him when you are bored or you need something because after a while you will start stirring something up in him. His logic gets to going, and it only makes sense that the reason you call on him is because you feel you can depend on him. And if you can depend on him you must like him. Every time he asks you to dinner you go, and you let him pay. I mean this just my story; I can only share with you what God gave to me.

Be in the right city so your man can find you; be among people who are like-minded. Now if you are reading this and you say I like being around the people who stand on the block, then please don't blame God when you get what you get. If you sit in the Devil's house long enough, you will get burned.

*****

Proverbs 31:24

"She makes linen garments and sells them, and supplies the merchants with sashes."
—Proverbs 31:24

"She makes linen garments and sells them, and supplies sashes for the merchants."
—Proverbs 31:24 KJV

*I*f you take a moment and really look at this verse, this speaks of the skill a Virtuous Woman has. In addition, her skill can be used in the workplace but also in her community for free. Let me break it down:

She makes fine linen and she sells them. This is her skill, making these garments, and from what God is telling us, this not just needle and thread. Now she is putting work into this and producing a great product, which brings her a profit. God has given us all a skill; no one is without one, but you have to tap into your skill. Some of us can handle money, working with numbers, like we can blink our eyes without giving it serious thought, and we find ourselves in job where we can play with numbers (budgeting, accounting, etc.). Then some of us are planners; we can plan an event from start to finish. God gives the vision, and we know what is needed to make the vision come into reality (wedding planner; event planner within job; etc.). Some of us are good at teaching others, whether it is children or adults. You just have a way of taking a task and breaking it down so others can understand it (School teachers, training monitors, etc.).

There are so many different skills women as a whole may possess. But there is one skill you have that you like to display because you know you are good at it. You enjoy doing it for anyone who is in need. As a matter of fact, if you happen to notice someone doing something wrong and you are good at it, if you don't help, you will sit back and critique the process the entire time.

All of these skills were given to us to assist with our day today living and gaining a profit. But it doesn't stop there ... How are you using your skill to glorify God?

"... and supplies the merchants with sashes." Between the definitions from Google and Merriam, to supply something means there is a need which can be fulfilled. So while you use your skill to pull in a profit, you should also be using your skill voluntarily.

God gave you something so you could use it to also glorify Him with it. The skill is not yours alone because it really belongs to God. The verse says a Virtuous Woman supplies the merchants; in other words she gives, contributes, provides, furnishes, donates, bestows, grants, endows, and imparts what she has to others. And from what God is telling me, in doing so there will not be an exchange of funds all the time.

Work it out in your mind I'll wait...

Ask yourself...
How am I giving?
How am I contributing?
How am I providing?
How am I furnishing?
How am I donating?
How am I bestowing?
How am I granting?
How am I endowing?

How am I imparting? Am I imparting it in a way which is pleasing to God? How does my skill bring glory to the Kingdom?

See God covered you because He ensured you could bring in revenue. But how are you covering Him with what He gave you. Please understand; it doesn't just start and stop with you giving our money to the church. You may be the person the church needs to help maintain finances for a little while or at least to impart the knowledge you have to someone else so they can do it.

You may be the person who has all these clothes with tags still on them that you don't ever touch, which means you are probably in a position to donate to those who don't have a closet to put clothes in. You try to get rid of old stuff so you can bring in the new, but you would rather throw it away, have a yard sale, or even give it to Goodwill for them to sell, rather than taking it to a shelter and or allowing the church to assist in furnishing their home.

When the pastor says we need volunteers to … What are you doing to contribute? Stop being so quick to throw out what you can't do or to say, "That's not me," and figure out what you can do to provide help and ultimately bring glory to the Kingdom.

"She makes linen garments and sells them, and supplies the merchants with sashes" (NIV).

You have a skill which brings you profit, and you should volunteer it to those in need.

*****

Proverbs 31:25

"Strength and honor are her clothing; and she shall rejoice in time to come."

—Proverbs 31:25 KVJ

*Y*ou know this woman, she is the one who you swear, "she thinks she perfect." But then you come to find out she is the real deal. It's doesn't seem like she has any issues; she doesn't have any drama. She always smiling and looks like she has never struggled a day in her life.

You know this woman; she can find the good in any situation. She is quick to tell you she will pray for you. Her advice is never really telling you what you should do, but she lets you know you should do something. She is more likely to lay out your options for you and share some of her story and how God brought her through. She empowers you to make your own decisions.

Some of us secretly don't like this woman because of what we see from the outside, looking in. But none of us really know her story, what she has truly been through, or how many times she has fallen and gotten back up—or how she had to reach out to her all mighty Father during those rough times when she felt all alone.

You know why you can't find no fault in her? You know why it seems like everything is perfect in her life? It is because she is in her safe place, in the arms of God her father. She has chosen to establish and maintain a relationship with Him. He is protecting her from those who seek to devour her. He is protecting her from the ways of the world. Why? What is it about her?

She understands God made a promise:

"If my people, which are called by my name, shall humble themselves, and pray, and seek my face, and turn from their wicked ways; then will I hear from heaven, and will forgive their sin, and will heal their land."
—2 Chronicles 7:14 KJV

She has repented:

"Have mercy on me, O God, according to your unfailing love; according to your great compassion blot out my transgressions. 2 Wash away all my iniquity and cleanse me from my sin."
—Psalm 51:1-2 KJV

She knows she is covered:

"Blessed is the one whose transgressions are forgiven, whose sins are covered.
Blessed is the one whose sin the Lord does not count against them and in whose spirit is no deceit."
—Psalms 32:1-2

She knows God has healed her land, and as long as she chooses to stand upright before the Lord all will be well. She understands she has a part to play in receiving the benefits of the promise God has made. I encourage you to read the entire chapters of all the verses given. Pray for understanding and that God reveals Himself to you in this word. Read the passage below and be blessed and encouraged.

If you feel like you are being attacked for no just cause and you need a breakthrough, I would encourage you to meditate on the passage above in addition to Psalm 35, and watch how God works.

When you choose to cover yourself in the promises of God and you stand upright before Him, He will hide you safely in His arms. Then strength and honor are your clothing, and you shall rejoice in time to come.

*****

Proverbs 31:26

"She speaks with wisdom, and faithful instruction is on her tongue."
—Proverbs 31:26

"She opens her mouth with wisdom, and the teaching of kindness is on her tongue."
—Proverbs 31:26 ESV

"She opens her mouth with wisdom, and on her tongue is the law of kindness."
—Proverbs 31:26 NKJV

"She openeth her mouth with wisdom; and in her tongue is the law of kindness."
—Proverbs 31:26 KJV

"When she speaks she has something worthwhile to say, and she always says it kindly."
—Proverbs 31:26 MSG

*Y*a'll ready? Here it is: Stop talking to hear the sound of your voice. Just because you have an opinion doesn't mean it needs to be heard. Let us be reminded *life and death* is in the power of *your* tongue. And if God didn't tell you to put in *His* sense in it, then you are probably speaking on the side of death.

Oftentimes in life we are in positions where our opinion holds weight. So for us moms, we don't have permission to say off-the-wall things to our children because we are their moms. We are still responsible for speaking, displaying, and imparting life and love into them. I know for myself, when I get real upset with my kids, I will start to talk just because I'm upset, and when I look back on it, I'm saying a whole bunch of nothing. So in essence what did I do? I wasted precious time in addition to breath, because my daughter probably checked out of the conversation after ten minutes.

Some of us are in positions of authority over others and because you can say jump you do, but there is no purpose. I recall a preacher say, "Are the words you speaking in love? Contrary to what you may think this applies to family, friends, coworkers, the poor man, the person who cut you off in line, the lady and her three kids who keep stopping in front of me in the grocery store, and the little child who has no manners."

I think you get the point.

Keep in mind that just because you have an opinion doesn't mean it is to be shared with others. We are so busy formulating our response to something that we may be missing what God has for us through what is being said. The acronym W.W.J.D. (What Would Jesus Do?) was not a trend. It should be our way of life, our way of thinking. Before you speak to something, know it is what Jesus would have you to say or do. Know that when you do, your words are planting seeds of life.

Momma said, "If you can't say anything nice don't say anything at all."

The Word says when my sheep hear my voice—this means you have established and are maintaining a relationship with our Father ... And I know them—God knows you because you have made yourself available to Him; by giving Him your life . . . And they follow me—you have submitted to His ways and not your ways (John 10:27). Simply put ...

She speaks with wisdom—when you speak there is a purpose.

"... and faithful instruction is on her tongue"—because you are actively desiring

God, it is expressed in love and it's lined up with the will and word of God.

*****

Proverbs 31:27

"She watches over the affairs of her household and does not eat the bread of idleness"
—Proverbs 31:27

This verse continues to tie in all the other things you have been told in the previous verses. You are supposed to make sure your household is maintained in every aspect. For example, I found out that I'm a painter. We wanted to paint our home. However, we could not afford it, and the more I looked around, the more I realized we needed to paint. Well, it is just like God for me to be watching shows which teach me how to maintain my home and the projects which may arise. By the grace of God I have managed to paint my home the way I wanted to at half the cost. Watching over the affairs of your home may mean you have to get off your butt and put in some work because that will be what is in the best interest of your household. For those of us with children, when we show our children how to work, and we allow them to assist us in projects, we are developing their character, building memories, and most of all sharing God's love with them.

She watches over the procedures—that means you have set ground rules in your home. God is not a man of confusion, but all things in which He is involved in is decent and in order.

She watches over action—this means you are ensuring the rules are being followed. It means you need to enforce the rules laid out. Don't compromise your walk with Christ because you don't want to lose a friend. As I heard someone say the other day, they don't have a Heaven or hell to put you in, so desire to please God.

She watches over objects—which means you are aware of what is coming in and out of your home. For those of us who have children. Please understand it is your responsibility to know they aren't building bombs in their rooms. For those of us who are single you should know if your friend has a habit of having illegal items on them which could cause you to be in trouble if not putting you in harm's way.

"... and does not eat the bread of idleness." The word *idle* means lacking worth or basis; vain, not occupied or employed; lazy. We should not be caught up in things which have no worth or meaning; we shouldn't be lazy. If it not pleasing to God and adding glory to His Kingdom, then you may not want to be in it. You should always be busy about doing God's work.

When someone keeps coming to you to gossip, learn to dismiss them or remove yourself from the situation because if the plan is not to help the person get through their situation, then you are wasting precious time. It lacks worth to stand and listen to gossip when you know you should be cleaning your home for no other reason than it needs to be done. Don't search for excuses to not get it done. Better yet, get in the habit of maintaining your home as if God is coming over soon.

Don't throw bricks at someone else's glass house when your house is made of glass, as well. Have you noticed the pattern?

God desires for His ladies to be productive in a positive things; He wants His woman to be about her business; in all we do, it should make God *look good*.

You know what I'm talking about, take it back. God *is* Mr. Right; everybody wants

Him and He knows it. Then the famous line, "Hey ladies, there's enough of me to go around." But really, there is enough of God to go around; all He wants is for you to make Him look good. God has already deposited in you what you need to make Him look good. God wants you to use your life in order to draw in others. Life is so much easier when we choose to rest in Him.

*****

Proverbs 31:28

"Her children arise and call her blessed; her husband also, and he praises her. Her children arise and call her blessed."

—Proverbs 31:28

So by now, you may be thinking what is the purpose of all this? The Virtuous Woman has a lot of responsibility, and that seems to be a lot of work. But believe it or not, God wants you to enjoy life here on earth as well as strive for your place in Heaven.

This life you choose to live as His Virtuous Woman brings glory to God's Kingdom and is full of rewards right here on earth. How rewarding is it when your child comes to you and gives you a kiss for no real reason, just because you are Mom. When your little one just crawls in the bed and lays on you. You may wonder what he or she is doing. But by the time they make themselves comfortable on you and all that love and compassion over comes you, you can't tell me that is not a great moment in your life. My husband often tells our children that when he has a bad day, he looks forward to hearing about their day. This reminds him that it is all worth it. I feel the same way when my kids are just playing, and I hear that hearty laugh between them; it makes my heart feel good.

This is a form of your children calling you blessed. See your children is a reflection of you, so if you step back and look at your life which includes your children and you say "it is well," then know that God is yet ensuring all is well. See, too often we are so concerned with what others think about us but are not concerned with what our children think of us.

What our children think is important for they will emulate what they see us do, say, and how we live for Christ.

But it doesn't stop there……her husband also, and he praises her. Self-explanatory right? The reality is so many of us take for granted how our husbands or how God calls us blessed and praises us. More often than not some women are not able to accept a compliment for what it is intended to be. We are quick to play down what has been said to us. "Baby I think you are beautiful" doesn't always mean they are trying to get us in the bed. The world has allowed us to think the good things come with bad intentions. Therefore, we are always looking for something to go wrong.

God allows for us to have moments for ourselves throughout our days. Those moments we touched on previously with our children. Sometimes, family will call out the blue just to say "I love you," and instead of assuming they want something from you, try saying thank you. Half the time, when someone you least expect reaches out to you, it's because God wants you to know it is in His power; all things are done. God gives us all that we need, though it may not look how we want it to. But if we stop long enough and reflect on the things we have been through, we see that it was God who brought us through; God made a way. God and we are still here today because He wants us to get it right with Him. As we mentioned before, it starts with a desire to do what God wants and then working at it every day.

Don't let the enemy take what God gives you and turn it around to doubt or an argument. But if all else fails in your thought process, God calls you blessed because you are reading this and since this is the day the Lord has made, you are blessed because He allowed you to see it.

*****

Proverbs 31:29

"Many women do noble things, but you surpass them all."
—Proverbs 31:29

"Many daughters have done virtuously, but thou excellest them all."
—Proverbs 31:29 KJV

"Many women have done excellently, but you surpass them all."
—Proverbs 31:29 ESV

"Many women have done wonderful things, but you've outclassed them all!"
—Proverbs 31:29 MSG

There are nice females in this world, and they accomplish what society deems to be amazing things. But, what does God say? If what you do and all that you have accomplished wasn't to glorify God, bring glory to the Kingdom in Heaven, or in the name of Jesus (the right way), then it was for nothing; it was in vain.

"What good will it be for someone to gain the whole world, yet forfeit their soul? Or what can anyone give in exchange for their soul?"
—Matthew 16:24–26

"For what is a man profited, if he shall gain the whole world, and lose his own soul? or what shall a man give in exchange for his soul?"
—Matthew 16:24–26 KJV

I like how the King James Version puts it, what do you profit? What will you gain; how does it benefit you? For you to have to world, and in the end your soul dies? Let take the pretty out of it ... How does the approval of the world benefit you if you die and live eternity in hell?

We have it confused or twisted if for one moment we think all we have to do is bring good to the world and all will be well. If you *fail* to acknowledge Lord Jesus Christ as your Lord and Savior, if you *fail* to get saved, if you *fail* to submit to your life to God our Father, if you *fail* to live the life God has called you to live which honors Him, then please know, understand, wrap your mind around it, and know the struggle is real: whoever is standing at the Heavenly Gates will *royally fail* ... to let you in.

The Bible talks about people who claim to do the good things in which God has command in the name of our Father. However, their words and the life they live don't match up.

"Not everyone who says to Me, "Lord, Lord," shall enter the kingdom of heaven, but he who does the will of My Father in heaven.

Many will say to Me in that day, "Lord, Lord, have we not prophesied in Your name, cast out demons in Your name, and done many wonders in Your name?"

And then I will declare to them, "I never knew you; depart from Me, you who practice lawlessness!""
—Matthew 7:21–23 KJV

I like The Message version which makes it a little plainer; it reads

Knowing the correct password—saying "Master, Master," for instance—isn't going to get you anywhere with me.

What is required is serious obedience—doing what my Father wills.

I can see it now—at the Final Judgment thousands strutting up to me and saying,

"Master, we preached the Message, we bashed the demons, our God-sponsored projects had everyone talking."

And do you know what I am going to say? "You missed the boat.

All you did was use me to make yourselves important. You don't impress me one bit. You're out of here."

As we break down whom this Virtuous Woman is, please know this person, this woman, this mother, this wife, is beyond valuable to God. He says no matter what good a woman does in this world, because you choose to be a Virtuous Woman who has sold out to the will of God and desires to please God in all you do, God deems you better than those who don't.

Think about it. When I was little we used to say "God says no higher." Whoever said this first won, there wasn't anything which could top saying "God says no higher." Nothing you could do or say would top what God says.

"Many women do noble things, but *you* surpass them all."—NIV

I pray we continue to actively work toward being the Virtuous Woman God calls us to be, knowing it will be worth it in the end—life eternally in Heaven.

*****

Proverbs 31:30

"Charm is deceptive, and beauty is fleeting; but a woman who fears the Lord is to be praised."
— Proverbs 31:30

"Favour is deceitful, and beauty is vain: but a woman that feareth the Lord, she shall be praised."
— Proverbs 31:30 KJV

"Charm is deceitful, and beauty is vain, but a woman who fears the Lord is to be praised."
— Proverbs 31:30 ESV

"Charm can mislead and beauty soon fades. The woman to be admired and praised is the woman who lives in the Fear-of-God."
— Proverbs 31:30 MSG

God sees through the fake people, those who are not genuine in their works. You know her; she is always smiling in someone's face, getting what she wants. You ask her to do something when the attention is not focused on her, and she won't even give it half a thought.

She acts like she is married to Satan himself when no one is looking, but when all eyes is on her she is just a cute as a button. She has no loyalty to any one person because she purposely rearranges her being to fit the crowd she is in.

If we understand charm as the act of pleasing others greatly by beauty and attractiveness, we'll find that God says it is deceitful, a lie, dishonest; it is deceptive, misleading, and unreliable. Above all, God says it won't last.

Oh, and the one who walks around like her feet only touches clouds and rose petals, her hair and nails stays done, and she looks like she stepped off the fashion magazine airbrushed and all: now I'm not saying as a woman you can't keep yourself looking presentable; however, what do you have that won't fade away? Where is your sustenance? Your endurance, support, genuineness—what will your legacy be? That you were pretty?

When my father was a recruiter for the military, I was his data entry person, and as we reviewed some of the test scores every so often he would say, "Man, I hope she is pretty." See at that time enlisting in the military was easy. All you needed was some sense to get in. But if your score was low to where you didn't qualify for any of the branches and you were a woman, my dad's hope was that you were pretty enough for someone to marry you so you could be taken care of.

However, even in that God says beauty is vain. So as time goes on, and we see it time and time again, if all you have is beauty, a man will one trade you in for another model; a man will invest his finances in to reconstructing you always; or a Man of God will try to encourage you to gain value. But oh, how precious it would be if you would start now and allow God to mold you into the woman He has called you to be.

Allow your legacy to be that you were a Virtuous Woman. Let your sustenance be of value to God our Father. But the only way to do that is to get in the word (Bible), commit to a church that God leads you to. Submit your life to Christ Jesus, and allow His ways to be your ways; let His will be done in your life. Think about it this way: if God has kept you this far in your life to where you were able to read this book, then think of just how great it would be if you decided to follow Him and His will for your life. If you think life is great right now without the covering of the almighty God, imagine just how great it would be with God's covering.

*****

Proverbs 31:31

"Honor her for all that her hands have done, and let her works bring her praise at the city gate."
—Proverbs 31:31

"Give her of the fruit of her hands, and let her works praise her in the gates."
—Proverbs 31:31 ESV

"Give her of the fruit of her hands, And let her own works praise her in the gates."
—Proverbs 31:31 NKJV

"Give her everything she deserves! Festoon her life with praises!"
—Proverbs 31:31 MSG

God has put a commandment out there for us to be "honored" for all that we have done. I like how the Message Bible says it: "Give her everything she deserves." The question now is, what do you deserve? What has your life's journey so far gotten you?

"Do not be deceived: God cannot be mocked. A man reaps what he sows. 8 Whoever sows to please their flesh, from the flesh will reap destruction; whoever sows to please the Spirit, from the Spirit will reap eternal life."
—Galatians 6:7–8

"Don't be misled: No one makes a fool of God. What a person plants, he will harvest. The person who plants selfishness, ignoring the needs of others—ignoring God!—harvests a crop of weeds. All he'll have to show for his life is weeds. But the one who plants in response to God, letting God's Spirit do the growth work in him, harvests a crop of real life, eternal life."
—Proverbs 31:31 MSG

While these are the same verses, but in two different translations, the bottom line is God is telling us yet again that you will get what you deserve.

You have heard, "there is honor among thieves," this is to say even within those who do wrong they still have a level of honor and respect for the corrupt system. Their behavior is validated by the responses of those who think highly of them. Let me clarify it a little bit more. I was in the "Single Moms club," we were strong women who don't need a man. I'm raising my kids, I have my own house, a job, and paying my own bills. I mean really, at that point my thought was, I only wanted a man for one thing, and even in that I had it taken care of. But I wanted a husband, specifically a man of God. Yeah I know, how was that going to work out, right?

However my friends and I stood strong together, still just as single as when we came out the womb, and I was asking God why I can't find a man of God? I can only imagine what God's faced looked like when He heard me over and over again. Then I heard it clear as day, "Rosalynn, you won't commit to me and my ways, so why would I give you a man of God?"

See, we would catch a guy, a nice guy even, build him up, and throw him back. And because we were leaning on each other so hard, there was no room for what God had in store for us.

What does this have to do with what you deserve? What does this have to do with honor among thieves, you ask? Well, we were stealing the hearts of these men. We were stealing their time; half the time I, at least, knew from day two that I wasn't interested. But because I didn't want to be alone, I strung the guy along. Then to top it all off, my friends condoned it. While they may not have actually said, "Hey you did a good job hurting him." They never told me I was wrong; as a matter of fact it went something like this. "You don't need him, girl; he wasn't on your level," "You are better off without him because you got this without a man." Well, how do I know if he was on my level or not when I didn't give him the time? While I may have this without him, I was the one asking God for a man. (I know, how does that work?) By acting in such a manner, I wasn't showing God I deserved a man of God.

But then life happened, and God allowed it to be so that I was isolated—no crew, no girls, no dudes hanging around investing in my beauty and charm (you know, those things God says is deceiving and fleeting). It seemed like family was even a no-show. So there I was, running back to God, asking the same ole question "God why …?" and I got the same answer. God, the Holy Spirit, Jesus Christ, and this Christian journey is not a game. God will not force you or me to choose Him. There is no such thing as a part-time Christian; you have to be all in with no plan "B." Either you're all in or you are all out. People love to say, God knows my heart. Yes He does, so He know when you are lying to yourself just like you know when you trying to justify your wrongs to yourself.

Just as you prove to God you can be committed to Him and His ways. You also are showing our Father you can handle submitting to a husband (a man of God).

Okay, so you may be thinking, I'm not desiring a husband. Don't change the fact, you should still be submitting to God so that you can receive the benefits of obeying God our Father, just as our parents would reward us for our good deeds. God wants to bless you in ways you could never imagine. You have to obey His will.

God loved us so much so, he gave us the Basic Instructions Before Leaving Earth (Bible) to assist the Holy Spirit in guiding us along this thing we call life. God knew we, as women, were going to have an identity crisis. So I believe he took the time out to ensure we as women knew what He said we are. Not only did God tell us in specifics to us as women. It lines up with everything else in the Bible.

"But as for you, O man of God, flee these things. Pursue righteousness, godliness, faith, love, steadfastness, gentleness. Fight the good

fight of the faith. Take hold of the eternal life to which you were called and about which you made the good confession in the presence of many witnesses."
—1 Timothy 6:11–12 ESV

"But you, Timothy, man of God: Run for your life from all this. Pursue a righteous life—a life of wonder, faith, love, steadiness, courtesy. Run hard and fast in the faith. Seize the eternal life, the life you were called to, the life you so fervently embraced in the presence of so many witnesses."
—1 Timothy 6:11–12 MSG

As you continue to desire God and strive to be the woman God has called you to be. Putting God first and developing a relationship with Him, will ultimately set the stage for success in all relationships you find yourself in. Remember a relationship is not just between you and a man, but it involves your children, parents, co-workers, friends, or people you meet in passing. These are all relationships and God will bless them if you "seek first the kingdom of God and His righteousness, and all these things (blessings) shall be added to you" (Matt. 6:33).

Bibliography

Scripture taken from *The Message*. Copyright © 1993, 1994, 1995, 1996, 2000, 2001, 2002. Used by permission of NavPress Publishing Group.

Scripture quotations are from the ESV® Bible (The Holy Bible, English Standard Version®), copyright © 2001 by Crossway, a publishing ministry of Good News Publishers. Used by permission. All rights reserved.

Scripture taken from the New King James Version®. Copyright © 1982 by Thomas Nelson. Used by permission. All rights reserved.